INVENTING
AMERICAN HISTORY

INVENTING AMERICAN HISTORY

William Hogeland

A Boston Review Book
THE MIT PRESS Cambridge, Mass. London, England

Copyright © 2009 William Hogeland

All rights reserved. No part of this book may be reproduced in any form by any electronic or mechanical means (including photocopying, recording, or information storage and retrieval) without permission in writing from the publisher.

MIT Press books may be purchased at special quantity discounts for business or sales promotional use. For information, please e-mail special_sales@mitpress.mit.edu or write to Special Sales Department, The MIT Press, 55 Hayward Street, Cambridge, MA 02142.

This book was set in Adobe Garamond by *Boston Review* and was printed and bound in the United States of America.

Library of Congress Cataloging-in-Publication Data

Hogeland, William.
  Inventing American history / William Hogeland.
    p. cm. — (Boston review books)
  ISBN 978-0-262-01288-1 (hardcover : alk. paper)
  1. Public history—United States—Case studies. 2. United States—Historiography. I. Title.
  E175.9.H64 2009
  973—dc22

                                        2008051250

10 9 8 7 6 5 4 3 2 1

To my brothers

CONTENTS

Preface ix
1 Inventing Alexander Hamilton 1
2 American Dreamers 45
3 Constitutional Conventions 89

PREFACE

EVERY SPRING VACATION IN THE EARLY TO mid-1960s, my mother took me and my brothers from New York City to Washington, D.C., and environs, where she had relatives. We were always excited to see the memorials and monuments again, walk along the Reflecting Pool, tour the Capitol, visit Mount Vernon. But we looked forward urgently to the National Historical Wax Museum.

The wax museum's thrills came from nothing more sophisticated than old-school verisimilitude. (It closed many years ago; no nine-year-old today would find it either thrilling or lifelike.) Dioramas pulled your fascinated gaze from the dark hallway. You looked closely at perfectly recaptured worlds. Even a historical event I found static and boring—President Jefferson signing papers to buy Louisiana—occurred in a room that vibrated with riveting authenticity. The dioramas were time machines, carrying you to places you could never have imagined so thoroughly on your own.

Imagining: that's what history seemed to be for. Subtlety was out. Every event was in progress at its crucial moment. Wilderness firelight revealed John Smith bound on his back, about to be tomahawked by a furious Indian while Pocahontas hurled herself forever between Smith and the poised weapon, her face full of conflicting passion. (Smith's chest was actually heaving up and down!) Theatricality, shared by all the dioramas, was heightened in the Ford Theater box, draped with bunting, where Booth pointed his pistol at Lincoln's back—you wished you could jump in, like Pocahontas, and stop him. The figures had high color, yet their color was individualized. They were warmblooded. General Macarthur waded on a hot beach in his boots and big sunglasses; out on the still Pacific horizon, a ship waited. John Brown stood on the gibbet. He stared right at you, wildly and vacantly unrepentant, the loop already around his neck.

My mother helped by telling us whatever we needed to know in order to take in the scene. No more, no less. We didn't need any coaching when a new diorama appeared, shortly after a new assassination. There were Mrs. Kennedy and the two kids our age. John-John was saluting in his coat and realistic little bare legs. My brothers and I reveled in that display as we reveled in everything else at the museum, and in all of Washington's cheap, fake history artifacts, the tri-corner hats, thin and easily dimpled, and corncob pipes (both were on sale at the Mount Vernon gift shop), along with colorful brochures we collected by the dozen without distinguishing categorically between one for Monticello and one for Luray Caverns. Unrestrained by such thing as carseats and seatbelts, we whined and scuffled in the back, watching for roadside historical markers.

My mother would almost always pull over and stop. We'd lean out and read the marker together, evaluate together the interest level of the event it marked. I can still taste my corncob pipe's plastic mouthpiece and smell the April air.

This book is about failings in what is sometimes called "public history"—the history we encounter in museums and tourist attractions, in newspaper columns and election campaigns, in public broadcasting and popular biographies. The wax museum traded in crude drama, lurid and sometimes apocryphal, greatest hits in conquest, expansion, war, and murder. Partly for that reason, it conveyed to a child the sense more of *realpolitik* than of manifest destiny. That Indian trying to kill John Smith seemed righteously angry, Smith only lucky. What grim times those were, when children could be brought to gaze on a perfect rendering of a presidential assassination only a year or two old. There was no happy summing up, no celebratory lesson. We didn't emerge into the sunlight with a feeing that the world had been made safe for democracy. From John Smith to John Kennedy, the story, unabashedly, was one of violence.

Public history must simplify. What I criticize here is not simplification itself but the kind of simplification that erases our deepest conflicts.

I didn't begin writing American history until after the terrorist attacks of 2001. When the first tower started to slide, we all knew that this was history, in the simplest and worst sense. Soon I was making my usual rounds, on my once-familiar lower-Manhattan streets, astonished by row on row of camouflaged soldiers, by detours around personnel carriers and tanks, smelling something I'd never smelled before. Imagination, mine and my country's, seemed to have failed.

I've been further astonished during the past seven years. A nonspecialist, and a sometime devotee of the wax museum, I've had a new desire to imagine our past, and a new desire to look closely at it. Public history should try to help all of us imagine and look closely. Too often it tries to do just the opposite.

WH
November 4, 2008

1
*Inventing
Alexander Hamilton*

Welcoming visitors to the U.S. Treasury Building's columned entrance, which faces Pennsylvania Avenue on the green edge of the National Mall, is a statue of Albert Gallatin. A Swiss-born sophisticate who was dandled as a child on Voltaire's knee, Gallatin served as the nation's fourth treasury secretary, first under Thomas Jefferson and then under James Madison. His statue was erected in 1947. For sixty years, Albert Gallatin has appeared to be the founding father of the Treasury Department.

Behind the building stands Alexander Hamilton. The first treasury secretary, Hamilton was for all practical purposes the creator of both modern American finance and the founding wealth of the United States. This is his house, by rights, and he'd be outraged to see his mortal enemy, whom he once tried to hang for treason, lording over its entrance while his own likeness is consigned to the back stairs.

Hamilton's weakened position came partly from changes in city planning: the original front is now the back. But Gallatin's symbolic prominence is no accident. The move to erect the statue began during the New Deal, when the Democratic Party was carrying on a romance with all things Jefferson. Great Depression–era Democrats identified the true founding not with the first election of 1788 but with that of 1800, when Jefferson's party beat Hamilton's, whose legacy New Dealers condemned as elitist and anti-democratic. There is irony in New Deal claims on Jefferson, who objected to Hamilton's policies precisely because they relied on the federal activism and central economic planning that FDR took to extremes. The party in power nonetheless carved Jefferson's face on the nickel and on a mountain, built him a big white memorial as opulent as Lincoln's and Washington's and, for decades in both public and academic history, pushed his reputation at the expense of Hamilton's. The injustice at the Treasury doors is only the lowest blow in a long fight to take Hamilton down.

Now, a Hamilton revival is not only under way but an accomplished fact. Wrestling anew with Hamilton's contributions to national politics and economics would be both fascinating and worthwhile. But neo-Hamiltonians, like the Jeffersonians of the '30s and '40s, have been chopping up the past to make it conform to their political aims. Hamilton's national vision and founding economics are far more troubling—so more compelling—than his promoters acknowledge. And because his promoters invoke Hamilton's legacy as a beacon for current policy, the emerging picture is a dangerous one.

The rehabilitated Hamilton was first presented to general readers in two biographies, Richard Brookhiser's slim *Alexander Hamilton: American* (1999) and Ron Chernow's best-selling tome, *Alexander Hamilton* (2004). The authors share a thesis: today's America is not Jeffersonian but Hamiltonian—a blend of high finance, central banking, federal strength, industrialization, and global power for which we are indebted to the rare imagination and existential derring-do of our founding treasury secretary. "The Man Who Made Modern America" is how Brookhiser put the idea in the subtitle of an exhibit he curated for the New-York Historical Society in 2004. Short on substance, long on gigantic videos of modern bridges and contemporary military training, and full of one-sided portrayals of Hamilton's critics as myopic and venal, the exhibit was lavishly produced and promoted as a blockbuster.

In 2007, Hamilton crossed all the way over to pop. The once "forgotten founder" became the subject of a PBS *American Experience* feature, which aired in the spring and is likely to live on in classrooms on DVD. Between scenes of bewigged actors reciting their characters' written prose in awkward soliloquy, Chernow and a raft of other historians relate an even more vaulting story than those told in the exhibit and the biographies. Some of the talking heads give Hamilton credit not only for founding the American financial system, but for the country's very nationhood.

There's a wonkish side to the Hamilton revival too. Certain policy writers, way ahead of the curve, have contributed to its torque, shooting Hamilton's legacy past history buffs and toward the halls of power. In 1997 David Brooks and William Kristol published a *Wall Street Journal* op-ed making an early case for what the authors called "national-greatness conservatism," a theme they'd been developing in articles for the *The Weekly Standard*, which Kristol helped found and where Brooks was senior editor. Looking for activist-government leaders that Republicans could love, they came up with Teddy Roosevelt, Henry Clay, and Alexander Hamilton—anything but bleeding-hearts of what Brooks and Kristol called "the nanny state"—who nevertheless saw an important role for the federal government in achieving ambitious national aims at home and abroad.

Since then, as Brooks has become a *New York Times* columnist and TV pundit, he's pressed the theme that Hamilton personifies national-greatness conservatism. In a major essay in *The New York Times Magazine* in 2004, he described Hamilton as author of a conservative tradition favoring limited government activism in service of social mobility and national unity. That year, he also raved up Chernow's biography in *The New York Times Book Review*. After September 11, pairing national greatness with Hamilton gained traction in right-wing policy circles. For the swearing-in of Treasury

Secretary Henry Paulson in 2006, President George W. Bush's speechwriters went out of their way to note the importance of Hamilton's legacy, and Paulson himself remarked that his father had been "a real Alexander Hamilton fan." The Hamilton cause drew financial support—for both the Historical Society exhibit and online components of the PBS special—from the Gilder-Lehrman Institute for American History, whose founders Richard Gilder and Lewis Lehrman have backgrounds in such conservative policy organizations as the Club for Growth and the Project for the New American Century.

Neo-conservative claims on Hamilton came to a head when Brooks, in a June 8, 2007 *New York Times* column on economic issues in the 2008 election, announced outright that he and like-minded others are "Hamiltonians," who hold the rational balance among radical populists, tinkering liberals, and knee-jerk anti-government conservatives.

Hamilton's reputation has bloomed on the liberal side, too, with the Brookings Institution's "Hamilton Project," which is dedicated to proposing "pragmatic policy responses that will create new opportunities for middle class affluence, bolster economic security, and spur more enduring growth." Emphasizing Hamilton's immigrant status and impoverished background, the project describes Hamilton as a representative of American traditions of opportunity and upward mobility. "Broken Contract," a widely discussed paper by the project's policy director Jason Bordoff, published in the September 2007 issue of *Democracy*, sets out an agenda clearly inspired by that vision of Hamilton. Bordoff argues that an essential promise of American democracy—parents who work hard and prize education can expect their children to advance economically—is in danger of being broken, and that extreme solutions coming from the left and the right will fail. He proposes maintaining mandatory forms of social insurance, making heavy investments in training and education, and increasing individual responsibility. The Hamilton Project's advisory council boasts Democratic Party luminaries such as Robert Rubin, Roger Altman, and others redolent of both the Clinton-era pragmatism and New Deal liberalism espoused by Bordoff.

That the Hamilton revival admits conservatives and liberals alike gives it obvious appeal. But if opinion-shapers really want to strengthen democracy by enhancing competition, opportunity, and mobility, Hamilton is not their man. Nor did he want to be. Neo-Hamiltonians of every kind are blotting out a defining feature of his thought, one that Hamilton himself insisted on throughout his turbulent career: the essential relationship between the concentration of national wealth and the obstruction of democracy through military force.

That's putting the matter bluntly, and bluntness is necessary. Time and again this galvanizing principle in Hamilton's political life has been denied, ignored, and glossed over by his proponents, who thereby distort the entire founding period. One can gain a refreshingly focused picture of Alexander Hamilton by looking at episodes in his public life, far from minor, that the rehabilitation industry's guiding storytellers have done their best to downplay or leave out all together. Among the most revealing is his participation in the dramatic events known as the Newburgh Crisis. Left out of the PBS biography, this affair launched the mature stage of Hamilton's relationship with George Washington and placed him for the first time at the center of public finance. It was nothing less than the formative experience in Hamilton's life as a political actor.

In 1782, fresh from serving as a battalion commander at the Battle of Yorktown, Hamilton, twenty-seven, joined the Confederation Congress as a delegate from New York and entered into a scheme to threaten the Congress with a military coup. As executed by the Congress's superintendent of finance (and Hamilton's finance mentor) Robert Morris, his assistant Gouverneur Morris (no relation), and Hamilton (their promising young protégé), the idea was to encourage Continental Army officers—deployed, after victory at Yorktown, in a cantonment at Newburgh, New York—to refuse to lay down their arms unless the states acquiesced in Robert Morris's longstanding insistence that the Articles of Confederation be amended to permit the collection of federal taxes from the whole American people. In Morris's plan, these taxes, collected not by weak state governments but by a cadre of powerful federal officers, would be earmarked for making hefty interest payments to wealthy financiers—including Morris himself, along with his friends and colleagues—who held millions of dollars in federal bonds, the blue-chip tier of domestic war debt.

The first tax Morris wanted Congress to pass was a duty on foreign goods, known then as an impost. Both Chernow and Brookhiser, for his part, focus exclusively on the impost. Morris, however, assured his supporters that once Americans were accustomed to paying federal tax, a slate of land taxes, poll taxes, and taxes on domestic products would soon follow. The idea, in Morris's phrase, was to "open the purses of the people" to enrich the interstate investor class, place American wealth in a few powerful hands, and create a unified nation, poised to become an empire.

The officers at Newburgh were disgruntled because, with the war effectively over, promises about pay and pensions had not been met (Morris routinely paid financiers before soldiers). When they sent a delegation to Congress to demand payment, Hamilton and the Morrises urged the officers to make common cause with the investor class by insisting on pay in federal bonds. Hamilton channeled Congress's panic about military takeover by insisting in resolutions from the floor that federal taxes be dedicated not just to officer pay but to funding all bondholders. He also took the immense risk—executed with remarkable coolness—of writing to Washington, on whose military staff he'd once served, to invite him to lead the threatened coup. But Washington's loyal officers spurned the Morrises' overtures, and when the conspirators in Congress reached out to Washington's enemy General Horatio Gates, a mutinous plan developed at the Newburgh camp to give Gates command of the army.

It was all quite a scene. The high point came at a meeting in Newburgh, where Washington leveraged his officers' affection to disable Gates, quell mutiny, and prevent takeover of Congress. Hamilton's correspondence during and after the crisis reveals a young man working assiduously to cover every bet. He subtly adjusted his solicitation of Washington when it became obvious the great man wouldn't play; he didn't scruple to criticize, even partly rat out, his fellow conspirators; and he confessed to Washington certain aspects of his own participation in the conspiracy, while covering up others. In one letter draft, he even crossed out a reference to having hoped, at least briefly, that the coup would actually occur. A reader of this richly entertaining bob-and-weave can only stand in awe of Hamilton's conjuring a role as Washington's congressional informant and confidant from participation in a treasonous conspiracy. He set up his entire career!

Certain aspects of the Newburgh Crisis are worth arguing about. (How willing were the Morrises and Hamilton to support an actual coup? Were they gambling on avoiding one at the last minute? How would they have controlled events if the Gates mutiny had succeeded?) What hasn't been at issue in any serious way, since E.J. Ferguson and Richard Kohn wrote about these events in the 1960s and '70s, is Hamilton's eagerness to avoid applying the rule of law to his view of what was best for the country. He had an urgent desire for an authoritarian government, whose well-funded debt, supported by nationally enforced taxes, would increase the wealth of the richest class of Americans and yoke that class to national purpose. He bet everything, including his reputation as a loyal patriot, on forging a common project between the military and the investor classes to override the will of elected governments.

Hamilton's gambit with the Morrises illuminates the style in which he would conduct his whole political career. So it is not surprising that both Chernow and Brookhiser usher readers hurriedly past Newburgh. Chernow's Newburgh narrative (which takes up only four of his 731 pages) omits the participation of Hamilton's all-important mentor Robert Morris, whose controversial, at times openly corrupt efforts of the 1780s were instrumental to Hamilton's successes in the 1790s. Chernow claims that Hamilton feared, rather than encouraged fear of, military outbreak, yet a few sentences later shows Hamilton "playing with combustible forces" by suggesting that Washington take the lead. Chernow characterizes Hamilton's writing to Washington as mere deviousness, which he excuses by noting that Gouverneur Morris (not identified by Chernow as Robert Morris's assistant) pursued the same stratagem with other officers.

Also without context in Chernow's rendering is the situation at the Newburgh camp itself, which somehow, inexplicably, grew "more incendiary": we do not learn that Robert Morris stoked the fire by offering Gates support for outright mutiny. Sustaining the distortion by quoting selectively from the Hamilton-Washington correspondence, Chernow describes Hamilton applauding Washington's judgment in quelling the coup. He persistently gives glimpses of Hamilton where glimpses favor him, snatches him out of sight where he is manifestly implicated, acknowledges a little naughtiness, and declines to tie the threads together.

The result is falsification of the Newburgh episode and a picture of Hamilton cleansed of all the existential daring, so outrageous and so troubling, that was the true source of his brilliance, and which would mark all of his later successes and failures.

Brookhiser makes the most dramatically revealing episode in Hamilton's early career disappear completely. His background on Newburgh consists of one sentence informing readers that the desire to raise money through federal taxes was motivated by a need to pay soldiers, implying that paying interest to creditors was a tertiary consideration necessary only to acquiring a foreign loan. Gone are the bondholders, whom Hamilton and Morris themselves told Congress were a primary consideration; paying foot soldiers was literally never an issue. Ferguson devoted a detailed book to Revolution-era finance, required reading for anyone trying to explain Hamilton, yet Brookhiser's only cited sources for his discussion of Newburgh are two of Hamilton's most enthusiastic, least probing earlier biographers.

The fuzziness that both biographers bring to pivotal moments like the Newburgh Crisis extends to the nature of the Revolutionary War debt itself, obscuring Hamilton's all-important relationship to it. Chernow claims that nationalists like Hamilton and Madison wanted to place Congress in a position to "retire the huge war debt." Precisely the opposite is true: led by Morris, the nationalists wanted, as they said repeatedly, to *fund* the debt—a distinction key to Hamilton's national vision and to the finance plan he carried through Congress at the dawn of the 1790s. Both in his book and in the PBS biography, Chernow treats the debt as something that, having been run up, somehow, to regrettable proportions during the war, confronted Hamilton as an unfortunate problem when he became treasury secretary. In fact, Hamilton had spent all his time in Congress, influenced by Morris and his own reading in finance theory, trying to protect and swell the debt. When he took office in Washington's cabinet, Hamilton brought years of effort to fruition at last.

Brookhiser doesn't say that Hamilton wanted to retire the debt, but his discussion of the funding plan again makes something disappear: the blue-chip tier of bonded debt held by Hamilton's and Morris's friends, on which Hamilton pinned all hopes for a powerful, unified nation. Brookhiser describes instead the kind of debt represented by the government's wartime IOUs, rehashing Madison's attempt to distinguish between chits still held by soldiers and farmers and chits that soldiers and farmers had already sold to speculators. But Ferguson, as well as Stanley Elkins and Eric McKitrick, in their magisterial *The Age of Federalism* (which Brookhiser cites elsewhere), showed years ago that the distinction between original holders and speculators was largely bogus and distracting. Hamilton certainly thought it was. That's because the most significant portion of the debt was held by few people and moved very little; speculators in lower tiers of debt included people like Morris and his cohort, who were also "original holders" of the best tier.

David Brooks does embrace the thrust of Hamilton's finance plan, writing that Congress's decision to fund the federal debt at Hamilton's urging formed the basis of "the fluid capital markets that are today the engine of world capitalism." The quick-and-dirty textbook version is that Hamilton gave the country sound credit. What that means is rarely made explicit: the first treasury secretary found ways to support, at all costs, the federal bondholders whom he and Morris had been frustrated in supporting in the 1780s. In 1791 Hamilton finally got the U.S. Congress to commit to paying reliable interest on its debt instruments, halting both their face-value depreciation and the free-for-all speculation in them, making them articles of rational trade in high-finance marketplaces.

(Following British models, Hamilton also used proceeds of the U.S. Post Office to create a "sinking fund"; such funds were dedicated to paying down each *issuance* of a public debt, making bonds reliable.) Hamilton's idea, bold and creative, was to let the government get its hands on easy money by letting bondholders and traders grow American fortunes lending that money.

Brooks also associates Hamilton's authorship of modern capitalism with what historians call "assumption." Hamilton persuaded Congress to assume the states' war debts in the federal one, thus swelling the federal obligation to massive proportions. But that idea wasn't original with Hamilton, and by overlooking its history, Brooks and other Hamiltonians obscure its purposes. Robert Morris, too, had wanted the Confederation Congress to assume state debts, placing all public debt in federal hands and making it so big that federal taxes would have to be levied to pay interest on it.

Hamilton was happy to report on Congress's inevitable deficit in December of 1790.

A NEW TAX, HAMILTON TOLD CONGRESS, was the only way to solvency. He proposed not only expanding duties on imports (the old, embattled impost had finally been passed in the first session) but far more significantly, imposing the first federal tax on an American product. Just as Morris had hoped, assumption of state debts had become the wedge for "opening the purses of the people"—enabling national taxation to support federal bondholders. In fact, passing the tax (on distilled liquor, a fact that has helped obscure its real purpose) was so important that in the first funding proposal he submitted to Congress Hamilton appended a fully drafted tax bill. It was characteristically Hamiltonian (and prescient of health-care-reform-era Hillary Clinton), replete with distilling and tax-policy minutiae and overwhelmingly, even patronizingly, thorough, with every loophole closed, every question pre-answered, every problem sure to be caused by Congress's financial ineptitude solved. The bill was controversial, and Hamilton's patience must have been tried when Congress, seeming to bumble, passed funding and assumption yet ignored the whiskey tax, the brilliant law that would pay for them. But he was becoming a politico. In reporting the deficit, he calmly referred Congress back to the tax law he'd written for them almost a year earlier. They were politicos too. They passed it—now that they had to—almost unmodified.

The structure of that tax undermines assertions made by Brooks and others that Hamilton wanted government power to enhance opportunity, mobility, and democracy. The reasons Hamilton gave Congress for going beyond a foreign impost and imposing domestic taxation are telling, both for what he said and for what he left unsaid. In the same 1790 report, Hamilton reminded Congress that merchants, naturally, paid import duties, and that since merchants had always been the class most committed to American nationhood, taxing them further would be onerous and disaffecting; hence the need for a new tax not on imports but on a domestic product. He did not point out that the merchant class was also the bondholding class. Bondholders had long been nationalists because federal power—the very kind Hamilton was wielding now—had long seemed to be where their interest (in every sense) lay. Today we might expect investors to be content with steady, tax-free income (there was, of course, no income tax). For Hamilton, shoring up bondholders' wealth meant paying that income with funds drawn not from the small bondholding class itself but from a tax collected from the large class of people who would never own a bond.

He promoted the financiers further by structuring the whiskey tax around aspects of the distilling process so that big-time distillers (industrialists, members of the bondholding class) would be charged a lower tax, while small-time producers (people engaged in a variety of work as farmers and artisans, with whiskeymaking often their sole source of cash and credit) would be charged a substantially higher tax, in many cases a crushing one. It was no accident. The bill was modeled on a series of whiskey taxes passed by British governments. Driving small and occasional producers out of business served imperial economic aims of efficiency and consolidation. In the same year that Congress passed Hamilton's whiskey tax, the Irish Parliament stopped merely "dis-incentivizing" small distilling, and made it actually illegal to operate a still of less than 500-gallon capacity.

Hamilton wanted to turn the country into an efficient global competitor. As he would argue before Congress in his famous 1791 "Report on Manufactures" (which was far less successful than his funding plan but just as eager to stun all comers with its depth of research on hemp, nails, hats—wool hats, fur hats, fur-and-wool hats—and so on), labor power should not be dissipated in small, generalist farms and one-man artisan shops but efficiently marshaled, stabilized, and deployed on commercial farms and in factory towns like the one he founded in Paterson, New Jersey. And he wanted to use federal power to achieve that great national vision.

The effect of the whiskey tax was indeed to render American distilling efficient, through consolidation bordering on cartelization. Even as the tax threatened to ruin small producers, Hamilton busily restructured army buying practices to make it impossible for smaller distillers to sell to army commissaries. In western Pennsylvania, where small distillers had managed to gain an economic toehold, Hamilton went even further: he awarded the job of federal tax collector to the region's richest, largest-scale distiller, a friend and crony of Washington himself. Paid both a federal salary and a commission on what he took from his less successful neighbors, charged with enforcing the federal tax that directly benefited his business, this distiller-collector had close relatives—again, federally commissioned, correspondents of both Hamilton and Washington—in the commissary office of the local army post. Business was thus sewn up.

Brooks routinely characterizes Hamilton's use of federal power as intended to spur competition and furnish opportunity. Yet control of business near the Ohio headwaters by a government-connected family and its pals was a direct consequence of Hamilton's policy, and it was anything but unintended. "Government is really bad at rigging or softening competition," Brooks has written by way of praising Hamilton's economic policies. The rigging in Hamilton's tax aggravated ordinary people's existing problems. Federally connected commercial farmers, big Eastern real-estate speculators, and entrepreneurs in brick, glass, iron, and other rising industries—the sort Hamilton always said he wanted to promote—bought up more and more of the best Western land. Farmers and artisans lost their weak grip on economic well-being and fell into massive foreclosure. Descendants of the pioneers who had cleared the land found themselves working as day laborers in the factories of their creditors. To Hamilton, that was anything but a bleak outcome.

Thus did the first federal domestic tax—linchpin to Hamilton's finance plan, culmination of nationalists' decade-long efforts to unite the country, first step in making the American economy a global competitor—operate regressively, comprehensively, and deliberately to restructure the country along the "modern American" lines now hymned by so many neo-Hamiltonians. Such extreme and systemic results can't be what Jason Bordoff and others at the Hamilton Project mean to support by invoking Hamilton's legacy. But it is what Robert Morris meant by opening the people's purses, and it's what Congress made law, at Hamilton's behest, in 1791.

In his 2007 *Times* column, Brooks pits his "Hamiltonians" against modern populists who want, he says, to "fundamentally rewrite the rules" and obstruct policies they see as benefiting only the rich. He would surely call populists the many former foot soldiers of the Revolution who rose up against the whiskey tax—the so-called whiskey rebels. To them, American independence seemed to have been gained for the exclusive benefit of a military-industrial cartel run for the privileged and staffed by the well-connected. Western Pennsylvania populists wanted a fair shot at "modern America" too. They wanted access to cash and credit. They wanted to grow their businesses. They were not anti-tax. They were against taxes that straitjacket markets, restrict opportunity, reduce competition, punish small operators, cripple local economies, and offer government cronies bonanzas at the direct expense of other citizens. Most important, they were against what they called taxes that didn't operate "in proportion to property."

At least that's what they said they were against, in published resolutions, letters, and petitions. Brookhiser and Chernow caricature them as drunk hillbillies (Brookhiser) whom scholars study merely because they are "colorful" (Chernow). But the fact remains that, during the nation's formative years, the idea that an essential promise of republican democracy lies in fostering opportunities for economic advancement and upward mobility is found not in Hamilton's funding plan, but in the resolutions of the ordinary people who rebelled against it.

So how have neo-Hamiltonians managed to remake Hamilton in their own image, diminishing his outrageous charisma and ruthless political intelligence in the process?

One way today's Hamiltonians connect their hero's economics to the American Dream is through the needle's eye of his disadvantaged background and remarkable success. "Hamilton came from nothing," Brooks wrote in his *New York Times Magazine* piece, "and spent his political career trying to create a world in which as many people as possible could replicate his amazing success." Or, as one of the PBS talking heads informs viewers, Hamilton believed that "if you worked hard, you should get ahead."

It's more likely that Hamilton believed exceptional bright-boys like him should erupt like meteors across the night sky. Blending creative genius with an almost mad degree of thoroughness and tenacity, he strove to dominate everyone he encountered, a quality that brought enormous success but also marred his life and may have shortened it. The idea that Hamilton spent his career trying to create conditions for replicating such a rise seems fantastic. One searches his letters and public statements in vain for thoughtful reflection on ordinary families' economic struggles or respect for their goals and hopes for their children's betterment. He appears unconcerned about using government power to encourage the rise of laborers' descendants and would not have related upward mobility to democracy—a dirty word to Hamilton.

Brooks cites remarks from "Report on Manufactures" as evidence of Hamilton's hope that people would advance socially by moving from agrarian scatteredness to industrial centralization. "When all the different kinds of industry obtain in a community," Hamilton argued, "each individual can find his proper element." He also defined as a goal of industrial policy "to cherish and stimulate the activity of the human mind, by multiplying the objects of enterprise." Where many founders were farmers and planters, Hamilton (like Benjamin Franklin and Samuel Adams) was an urbanite, and he made an appealing case for the creative synergy to be found in cities. He certainly wanted people "mobile" enough to get off the farm, out of the artisan shop, and into the mill.

But it is a feat of intellectual acrobatics to ascribe to Hamilton, on the basis of these remarks, a broad policy of encouraging, much less sustaining, widespread upward social mobility through hard work among succeeding American generations. For Hamilton, the "hard work/get ahead" equation, which revivalists want to call a democratic legacy, applied only to the sort of people he deemed it wise to encourage. He had cogent national and financial reasons for carefully dismantling the few ways—which already involved manufacturing and selling—that ordinary people had of getting ahead. His methods involved consolidating land, money, opportunity, and power in the West, while obstructing both mobility and democracy.

Chernow, straining to detect some sympathy in Hamilton for the impossible difficulties faced by the debtor class, misreads a minor *Federalist* essay, number six. He suggests that Hamilton felt sorry for Daniel Shays, leader of a 1787 debtor uprising in Massachusetts, and suggests that federal assumption of state debts was intended to relieve small-farming debtors. While it's true that Hamilton objected to vacillations from leniency to aggressiveness in Massachusetts finance policy, his essay as a whole makes clear his disdain for the vaunting ambition and criminal tendencies of all such as Shays, on whom he lays personal blame for the anti-creditor movement sweeping the western part of the country, the real basis and wide scope of which Hamilton always impatiently declined to acknowledge.

To the extent that he thought about it at all, Hamilton wanted people to stop talking nonsense about their own economic aspirations and get ahead his way and his way alone, by becoming efficiently organized laborers and farm workers for the financiers and industrialists. If people wouldn't do that, he'd make them.

Wanting to get ahead in their own ways, and seeing Hamilton's economic policy menacing the unalienable right to the political and economic participation they'd suffered for, the whiskey rebels crossed the line and became criminals. Hamilton crossed that line too—with a vengeance. He revived what some might prefer to write off as his youthful fling with militarism at Newburgh.

The rebels, fatally romanticized by both progressive and libertarian historians, were militarists too. They tortured and terrorized officials and civilians, took over militias and courts in western Pennsylvania, marched against soldiers of the U.S. Army, came close to burning Pittsburgh, purged the region of undesirable citizens, and threatened the union with secession. Salient to understanding Hamilton is how he chose to interpret those threats and frame the government's response. Long before the rebels took military action, Hamilton was eager to define what were then only a few, scattered crimes as acts of war. He pressured Washington to subdue, police, and occupy the entire area with overwhelming force. Frustrated by cabinet moderates' insistence on due process, as set out in the Bill of Rights, Hamilton worked with allies in the attorney general's office to serve summonses that he knew would fan the flames of rebellion, overriding new rules by which Congress was trying to remove inflammatory provisions.

When matters reached a fevered pitch in the summer of 1794, Attorney General William Bradford engaged in sham negotiations with the rebels to buy time for a secret military buildup run by Hamilton, who had eagerly volunteered to lead the mission. To sustain the false impression that the government sought a peaceful resolution to the conflict, Hamilton told Henry Lee, governor of Virginia, to postdate orders calling out the Virginia militia. When the buildup was complete, Hamilton took command of a 20,000-troop operation. His letters to Washington managing that sleight-of-hand (he'd been confirmed by the Senate to manage the Treasury Department, not to wage war or police the citizenry) make fascinating reading. Washington wisely led the troops only part of the way, then turned back, leaving the dirty work to Hamilton.

Citizens throughout Western Pennsylvania were subjected to door-kicking mass arrest and round-up, at Hamilton's behest, on what he knew—even, at times, said—was no evidence. The writ of habeas corpus was not suspended, as required in such cases by the Constitution, yet men were detained by the hundreds without charge and for indefinite periods. They were threatened with worse punishment, at times personally by Hamilton, in an effort to extract false testimony against other citizens.

The judicial branch was explicitly subordinated to military authority, and the federal judge who accompanied the troops—craven at best, probably a willing collaborator—said later that he'd charged some detainees despite insufficient evidence, fearing for his own safety at the hands of the troops.

That juries convicted almost none of the men who were marched across the mountains to Philadelphia in the middle of winter (some of whom hadn't even been charged) and then left for months in jail awaiting trial, has been taken—by cockeyed optimists—as a victory for the jury system. That reading ignores Hamilton's purposes, which had nothing to do with trying legal cases and achieving convictions. His letters to Washington, who grumbled about Hamilton's failure to capture legitimate suspects, are a primer in goal-shifting. Having at first assured Washington that the adventure was worth undertaking because many such suspects would be captured, Hamilton airily dismissed the issue when they weren't, and he refocused Washington's attention on the necessity of leaving an occupying force in the region to prevent further outbreaks. That occupation subjected law-abiding citizens, who had already been terrorized by the rebels, to martial law. Soldiers went from house to house confiscating scarce food and supplies and administering loyalty oaths.

Contemporary accounts and affidavits make clear that some of the testimony Hamilton tried to extract from detainees was intended for use not against the rebels, but against Hamilton's political enemies William Findley and Albert Gallatin, elected representatives who acted as moderating influences—at great personal risk—during the rebellion. Hamilton hoped to use the false evidence to silence his political opponents by hanging them for treason.

Unleashed, the existential hero was in a white heat. Using the military to trounce the rule of law and violate civil rights was integral to his vision of federal power, national wealth, and a strong union.

The historian Joseph Ellis, in *Founding Brothers*, is one of the few recent popular writers on the founding period who take a clear-eyed look at the latter phase of Hamilton's career, which began with suppressing western Pennsylvania. He cites the all-important source Richard Kohn, concluding that Hamilton's success in the Whiskey Rebellion inspired an almost obsessive military focus as he grew older. Out of office, Hamilton continued to order around his shadow-government hacks in the Adams cabinet (or as the PBS biography puts it, he "advised" them), hoping to contrive all-out war with France. Hamilton envisioned leading the U.S. army into Spanish Florida, then continuing into Central and South America. In response to the Kentucky and Virginia Resolutions, which denied the supremacy of the federal government, he suggested putting the entire state of Virginia "to the test" militarily, something his fans write off as mere venting and posturing, but which Ellis takes seriously.

Hamilton is routinely credited as favoring a strong executive branch. What he really favored, from Newburgh through the Whiskey Rebellion, from the quasi-war with France through his response to the anti-federalism of the Kentucky and Virginia Resolutions, was an executive branch run by him, strong enough to do anything it deemed in the national interest. For Hamilton, personal and military force—unrestrained by the slightest consideration of law—were joined ineluctably to American wealth, American unity, and American modernity.

2
American Dreamers

The eighty-nine-year-old musician and activist Pete Seeger, who is largely responsible for connecting folk music to the American left, joined the Communist Party in his twenties. Seeger has been candid, if at times self-serving, about his early support for Stalin, but the recent PBS *American Masters* documentary on Seeger is so disingenuous, when it comes to his and the Party's activities, that it gives an impression of 1930s communism as a program for nothing more than peace, equality, and down-home music. The young Seeger comes across as a cheerleader not for Stalin's Russia, but only for the sorts of social reforms any progressive might advance today.

Equally misleading in its portrayal of an unsettling early position has been press coverage of the career of William F. Buckley, Jr., who died in February of last year. Buckley made his name by providing intellectual leadership to those who did much, in the 1940s and '50s, to punish Seeger, other former Party members, fellow-traveling liberals, and certain bystanders. Appreciations of Buckley's contribution to conservatism blur not his embrace of McCarthyism—some of his admirers remain fairly proud of that—but his support for white Southern efforts to prevent black citizens from voting.

Buckley and Seeger share, along with fake-sounding accents and preppie backgrounds, a problem that inspires forgetfulness, falsification, and denial in their supporters. Fired by opposed and equally fervent political passions, both men once took actions that their cultural progeny find untenable.

Yet these two men—their careers strangely linked in the hunt for communists, the struggle for equal rights, and the emerging "culture wars" of the postwar era—are worthy of consideration without air-brushing. Their names alone may evoke, for those who lived through it, the anxiety and turmoil that marked American cultural and political life during the Cold War. Mutual hostility between Seeger types and Buckley types devolved on fears of imminent, world-ending invasions; plans for preventing evil from ever recurring on a mass scale; and stark disagreements over what is legitimately American. When the Soviet Union was annexing its neighbors, filling gulags, and making swaggering predictions of world dominance, and the United States was toppling elected leaders in favor of authoritarians and hounding domestic dissenters, all amid the stockpiling of nuclear weapons, the division among Americans could feel, to those on both sides, like the last battle for humanity. What Seeger's and Buckley's youthful actions meant in their time, deliberately obscured by today's lionizers, means something crucial now.

Pete Seeger inherited communism from his father. That decisive event in the history of American vernacular music has no place in the *American Masters* documentary. Charles Seeger, an arch-WASP bohemian born in 1886, taught musicology at Harvard and Berkeley. During his time in California, he formed an alliance with the Industrial Workers of the World, or Wobblies, an especially lively labor-organizing effort, which planned global working-class takeover through one vast, general strike. Soon, like many others, he was connecting his radicalism to the more tangible success of the Marxist revolution in Russia. He joined the Communist Party and started a radical group called, in the exciting new lingo, the Composers Collective, which encouraged pieces by left composers like Aaron Copland and Marc Blitzstein and published a magazine called *Musical Vanguard*.

American leftists like Charles Seeger did not interpret the expression "international communism" to mean "Soviet dictatorship and expansion." They saw the young Soviet state as the first in a series of concerted revolutions through which workers would take ownership of the means of production and humankind would advance toward a future without the awful poverty that was destroying the lives of so many laborers, blacks, and poor people in America and elsewhere. American communists wanted to build a homegrown movement that would bring together factory laborers, dirt farmers, mineworkers, fruit pickers, and sharecroppers. They hoped to shatter elite privilege, end race discrimination, and distribute fairly the wealth of the United States and the world.

Charles Seeger also wanted to connect Marx-Leninism to his own discipline. The Wobblies were famous for singing on picket lines, but Seeger was trained in the high classical tradition and called at first for modernist concert pieces—in a Soviet official-culture vein—celebrating the workers' collective virtue.

He wrote articles on music theory for *The Daily Worker*, the paper through which the Party updated communists and sympathizers on Communist International, or Comintern, policy. But by the late 1920s—and especially in partnership with his second wife, the composer and musicologist Ruth Crawford Seeger—he began seeing in traditional American music an art form already owned by the masses. Folk music, Seeger thought, existed outside the corruption and alienation of bourgeois culture; it needed only integration with Party ideology to become a means of worker empowerment. By the late 1930s—when his son Pete was becoming a politically passionate Harvard student, and the Great Depression was deepening American leftists' desire for change—the elder Seeger was discovering much of value in old ballads, work songs, blues, and traditional dance music, still thriving mainly in the South.

The American folk revival was not, however, the exclusive province of the left. In Europe, folk collecting and the promotion of traditional arts had long been emblematic of nationalist patriotism. In the United States, an early promoter of folk music was the inveterate reactionary Henry Ford, who saw the music as unsullied by the immigrant and urban cultures he despised and the salaciousness he associated with jazz and vaudeville. American folk music and dance—which Ford believed, fancifully, to be essentially Anglo-Saxon—would be the musical component of the hygienic culture he wanted to promote among workers in factory towns, places where, for the supposed good of the workers and company efficiency, everything from labor to education to recreation was to be controlled and supported by the owner. To that end, Ford encouraged the first fiddlers' contests, community sings, and square dances from which an important strain of the American folk revival emerged.

For leftists, too, folk music seemed free of corruption, but that meant free of Ford-style mass production, which was, in their view, oppressive in a way that Soviet mass production was not. To them, radio pop seemed aesthetically vapid and socially regressive. Old songs and tunes, which some of today's folkies still imagine being handed down from time immemorial in backcountry communities, seemed to embody the inherently cooperative spirit of the people, a natural sense of union.

Yet most of the music heard in homes in the Southern backcountry actually had roots in commercial pop—the medicine and minstrel shows, Tin Pan Alley, Victorian parlor sheet music, ragtime and jazz, and, by the 1930s, downmarket "race" and "hillbilly" seventy-eight-rpm recordings and clear-channel broadcasts of "barn dance" radio shows. The genius of people living in neglected parts of the country often lay in adapting pop music to cheap, sometimes-handmade instruments and whooping it up. One can only wonder what the bottleneck-guitar-picking sharecropper or the fiddling miner, steeped in a fecund mixture of tradition and commercialism old and new, might make of the arrival of a left-wing academic, complete with notepad and giant tape recorder, eager to preserve Southern music's supposed timeless purity.

That strange relationship between homemade music and left politics was further complicated in the 1930s by changes in both the U.S. government and the Comintern. In 1935 Stalin announced "The Popular Front"—a worldwide coalition of communism with liberal politics that the Party had formerly excoriated. A goal was to restrain the expansion of Germany against Russia at any cost. *The Daily Worker* started encouraging communists to collaborate with liberals. Many leftists—some of whom were disaffected by Stalin's nationalism and dictatorship in Russia—found a place in the New Deal government. Among them were Charles Seeger and Alan Lomax, a left-wing folklorist who gave Pete Seeger a job at the Library of Congress.

But in 1939 Stalin made a nonaggression pact with Hitler and repealed the Popular Front, leading many to flee the Party in disgust at the alliance with fascism. In this new ideological environment, Pete Seeger's career blossomed. Having traveled in the South and become adept at five-string banjo, the younger Seeger put his folk music to the service of the new Party line, which now opposed New Deal liberalism and U.S. war against Germany. In 1940 and '41, with the approval and guidance of Party elders (against whose dictates Seeger sometimes chafed), the group that would become known as the Almanac Singers, most notably featuring Seeger on banjo and Woody Guthrie on guitar, yoked "people's songs" to the Party agenda in a way that neither the philosophy of Charles Seeger, nor the musicians of the Southern backcountry, ever could.

As stars of Party-inspired organizing, playing for strikers and at New York rent parties, the Almanac Singers invented the music that leftists had failed to find among the actual folk. They gave the old songs new lyrics, celebrating unions and mocking FDR as a warmonger. (In his book *Where Have All the Flowers Gone*, Seeger is refreshingly self-deprecating about his "peace" verses' doggerel and thin satire.) They began the vogue for wearing work clothes—overalls, jeans, denim shirts—to denote membership in the people. According to Joe Klein, in his definitive biography of Woody Guthrie, they even adopted fake Southern accents and concocted biographies of hard travel. Most importantly for American music, the Almanacs invested their sound, which was far smoother than the real thing, with a mood of authenticity that the real thing never aspired to. Heads thrown back and mouths wide open, strumming and "singing out" with rousing, clean-cut intensity, they conjured a communist American future based on a fantasy of the rural American past.

Seeger was playing a rent party in June of 1941 when somebody rushed in with the news:

Germany had invaded Russia. The pact was broken. Another reversal of the Party line immediately ensued. To the relief and bemusement of the Almanacs, they were now required to sing against Hitler. But they were also required to ally with Churchill, whom the Party had been calling an irredeemable imperialist. In his book, Seeger recalls his hilariously rushed conversation with Guthrie about how to adjust to supporting Churchill. "'Why, Churchill said "All support to the gallant Soviet allied!"' 'Is this the same guy who said twenty years ago, "We must strangle the Bloshevik infant in its cradle!"?' 'Yep. Churchill's changed. We got to!'" Seeger, Guthrie, and the Almanacs started writing and singing pro-war songs full of glib jingoism that may have surpassed, for sheer dumbness, their anti-war ditties: "Round and round Hitler's grave / Round and round I go."

For six months, the group rallied the United States to enter the war, per the Party line. Then, with the bombing of Pearl Harbor in December and the declaration of war, they began singing rah-rah songs for victory. Soon Seeger was in the Army and Guthrie was a merchant mariner and the prewar phase of Seeger's career, and of the American folk revival, came to an end.

The major theme of the documentary is the lifelong connection between Seeger's music and his social activism. Yet it erases that connection's formative moment—formative not only for Seeger, but also for leftist politics and American music. Even a passing reference to Charles Seeger's radicalism would seem pertinent to Pete Seeger's early development as both artist and activist. Truly disastrous, though, are the few moments that do purport to deal with Pete Seeger's communism. We see footage of Hitler, and then see Seeger, in a recent interview, recalling collegiate arguments over what to do about Nazism. Some argued for pacifism, Seeger says, but "communists said the whole world should quarantine the aggressor. And I thought they were right." Snippets of Seeger's interviews then get stitched into a hasty, deliberately vacuous summary of his Party activities. Over a still of an "International of Youth" pamphlet, which gives way to a shot of Harvard's gates, Seeger's voiceover runs: "I ended up joining the Young Communist League, and let my marks slip, and I lost my scholarship to Harvard. Few years later,"—now over a still of young Seeger playing for a dance, with a group singing "Solidarity Forever" in the background—"just before World War Two, I think I—" cutting back to Seeger being interviewed "—actually joined and became a card-carrying member." Over footage of communist picketers, he says: "I was against race discrimination, and Communists were against race discrimination. I was in favor of unions, and Communists were in favor of unions."

That's pretty much all the film has to say about the role of communism and global politics in Seeger's early career. The Almanac Singers are introduced over stills of handbills for their performances (one reads "leading American Balladeers in a program of songs for peace"), followed by a still of the group itself, with Seeger saying in choppy voiceover: "The goal of the Almanacs—if anybody asks us— 'we want to build a singing labor movement.' But we'd barely got started on that job before World War Two broke out." Then, over a still of people reading about the Pearl Harbor attack in newspapers and a faint, crackling voiceover saying "Remember Pearl Harbor," Seeger says, "All the idea of strikes and everything [a cut or a mumble], 'after the war is won, then we can think about that.'"

In the edit, there is no mention of the Party's decisive role, which had Seeger singing against the war and then had him singing in favor of it well before Pearl Harbor, which the edit brazenly presents as the cause of Seeger's change of heart. Nor is there any mention of Stalin or the pact, although Seeger himself has not been afraid to discuss these issues before. When he says, for example, that the communists wanted to quarantine Hitler, he is probably reviving an argument he made in his book: the great powers were actually hoping Hitler would knock out communist Russia; when ambassador Litvinov asked in the late 1930s for a plan to bottle Hitler up, the liberal democracies turned their backs. While some might take a more critical view of Stalin's hope for quarantine, in the book Seeger is making a point with a basis in fact. An authorized biography by David King Dunaway (who appears as a talking head in the film) presents the young Seeger as unhappy about the pact but taking a "wait-and-see attitude." As recently as 2007, in a widely published letter to the conservative Ronald Radosh, Seeger discussed his delusions about Stalin.

In the film Seeger's comments become meaningless. His declaration that strikes would have to wait until after the war only makes sense in a context that the film cannot give, as doing so would reveal Seeger's again tailoring his music to Communist Party instructions. When FDR asked U.S. labor unions for a wartime no-strike pledge, the non-communist part of organized labor gave it. Significant for Seeger's career is that the Comintern sent word to the radical end of the labor movement to support the no-strike pledge too. Seeger might have had something interesting to say about ambiguities in Party labor policy. Dunaway's biography suggests that he found the Party's support for the no-strike pledge frustrating: strikers were a key Almanacs audience.

What Seeger has said before about the Almanacs' anti-war stance, the knee-jerk relationship to Party prescriptions, and his own support of Stalin are all absent. Cleansing the story of anything possibly upsetting or even nuanced, the filmmakers must be hoping to certify Seeger, despite former Soviet attachments, as an unimpeachably great American cultural figure of the kind often celebrated on PBS *American Masters*. Gained at the cost of falsehood, certification not only does no good, it weakens our grasp on the truth. There probably will not be another well-funded, closely researched, carefully edited, widely broadcast documentary on Pete Seeger, complete with interviews. This one has failed each of the astonishing things it pretends to celebrate: the folk revival, American activists' passions, the past century's idealisms, and the long, strange career of Pete Seeger.

WILLIAM F. BUCKLEY, JR., WHO DIED LAST year at eighty-two, enjoyed a busy and influential career as the most famous galvanizer of American conservative thought. Buckley made *National Review*—the magazine he founded, edited, and published—a kind of think tank for postwar conservative ideology. In its pages, he and his ideological compatriots championed strictly limited government, assertive law enforcement, rollback of the welfare state, free markets, and ceaseless war on communism at home and abroad. As a result, friends and foes alike have credited him lately with ending liberalism's intellectual hegemony, which prevailed in the U.S. political establishment from FDR's accession in 1932 until 1968, the bitter end of the Johnson administration.

The young Buckley's hopes lay partly in knocking out the then-vibrant liberal wing of the Republican Party. As George Will, one of the many leading conservative writers who once worked at *National Review*, eulogized him in *The Washington Post*:

> Before there could be Ronald Reagan's presidency, there had to be Barry Goldwater's candidacy. It made conservatism confident and placed the Republican Party in the hands of its adherents. Before there could be Goldwater's insurgency, there had to be *National Review* magazine.

The acceleration of conservatism involves an irony: in the magazine's widely quoted inaugural essay, Buckley described the publication standing "athwart history, yelling Stop." He wanted to stop the modern tendency of government to engage in what he called "radical social experimentation" in the form of such things as the New Deal and the United Nations, which he saw as products of a moral relativism that had become monolithic in the halls of American power. What he most wanted to stop was tolerance for what he considered modern error's extreme form, the Marx-Leninist view of humanity's advancement, through philosophically discernible stages, toward a condition of perfect equality fostered by an all-powerful state. Like Charles and Pete Seeger, Buckley looked to the Soviet Union as the fulfillment of an idea—one that he called satanic.

Buckley often referred to the Soviet empire by a single word, "gulag." On TV in the

1960s and '70s he'd purr the second syllable, eyebrows shooting past his hairline to show-stopping effect. By then, almost everybody was looking at the Soviet Union in moods ranging from concern to fear and loathing. Even Pete Seeger quit the Communist Party in the late 1940s. He and much of his prewar cohort had grown painfully aware of the awful oppression imposed on Russians and more and more Europeans. The Iron Curtain, as Churchill dubbed it, had fallen; the nuclear buildup had begun; Soviet tanks had rolled. International communism now meant, flagrantly, Soviet takeover of the world, including, in the famous words of President Khrushchev, the grandchildren of Americans. Today, Khrushchev's words may seem defensive braggadocio. Few took them that way at the time.

To Buckley and likeminded others, the socialist threat to American liberty lay not only in massive programs like Social Security, but also in the New Deal practice of giving government jobs to semi-secret communists and more open "fellow travelers"—the Alan Lomaxes and Charles and Pete Seegers and, even more seriously, their counterparts in sectors involving national security. After the war, communists were officially included among subversives seeking to bring, in the words of the McCarran Act of 1950, "totalitarian dictatorship" to the United States. Party members and others had long been eagerly accepting instructions for domestic revolution from a police state with which the United States now verged on what seemed a war for the future of humanity. Having quit the Party was no defense; hence the famous question, "Are you now or have you ever been . . . ?" Despite his avowed reservations about Senator Joseph McCarthy, the young Buckley gave strong support, as did much of the liberal establishment (in Buckley's view weakly and perhaps insincerely), for what McCarthy and the House Un-American Activities Committee defined as a hunt for Russian spies,

Party members, and communist sympathizers in government, entertainment, the arts, and business.

Buckley's inaugural essay for *National Review* ascribed such great and entrenched power to liberalism, and such frailty to nascent conservatism, that even small successes could be greeted with shouts of astonished joy. And few would now deem conservative successes small. While welfare and entitlement programs that Buckleyites attacked appear likely to survive, the ambitious young Buckley of the 1950s turned out to be on, and to play a part in determining, what some consider the winning side of history.

But in one area—the civil rights movement—Buckley conservatives were decisively not on the winning side. "Why the South Must Prevail" is the title of a 1957 editorial by Buckley addressing efforts to enforce federal laws ensuring blacks the ability to vote. The piece argued in part:

The NAACP and others insist that the Negroes as a unit want integrated schools. Others disagree, contending that most Negroes approve the social separation of the races. What if the NAACP is correct, and the matter comes to a vote in a community in which Negroes predominate? The Negroes would, according to democratic processes, win the election; but that is the kind of situation the White community will not permit. The White community will not count the marginal Negro vote. The man who didn't count it will be hauled up before a jury, he will plead not guilty, and the jury, upon deliberation, will find him not guilty. A federal judge, in a similar situation, might find the defendant guilty, a judgment which would affirm the law and conform with the relevant political abstractions, but whose consequences might be violent and anarchistic.

The central question that emerges—and it is not a parliamentary question or a question that is answered by merely consulting a catalogue of the rights of American citizens, born Equal—is whether the White community in

> the South is entitled to take such measures as are necessary to prevail, politically and culturally, in areas in which it does not predominate numerically? The sobering answer is Yes—the White community is so entitled because, for the time being, it is the advanced race.

At the time, Buckley had been editing *National Review* for only two years, having founded his magazine at twenty-nine. Though the editorial is unsigned, there can be little doubt that it is his work. Editorial policy was his domain; more tellingly, its idiosyncratic blend of elegance and provocation was already becoming a Buckley trademark.

National Review would reject the very term "civil rights movement" as "ludicrous," insisting instead on "the Negro revolt" as late as 1964. Not only did the effort to keep blacks from voting fail, Buckley's carefully articulated justification for illegally denying them the vote failed too, so utterly that today's Buckleyites, celebrating the great sweep of the man's pervasive influence, can't seem to recall a thing about it.

The *New York Times* obituary did mention, briefly, that Buckley supported the segregationist South on the grounds of white cultural superiority. More typical of mainstream assessment was the long summation of Buckley's career in *Newsweek*, which said only that Buckley "tolerated" segregation and supported white Southerners' "protesting." That characterization, misleading in its vagueness, softens the conservative position on integration—the defining issue of the day, along with the Cold War. Readers of recent articles on Buckley's career could be forgiven for having no idea that *National Review* described Martin Luther King, Jr. as a "rabble-rousing demagogue" who taught "anarchy and chaos" or that it identified integration with Soviet communism.

The more textured, less temperate discussion of Buckley's politics developed online, where some bloggers and commenters loudly celebrated Buckley's death as the end of an evil phony, whom some called, among other things, a racist, citing part of the '57 editorial. Buckley fans responded that the civil rights position was a glaring exception to a tough, not bigoted program; that the position amounted to states-rights advocacy, not racism; that Buckley later took a more enlightened view (*Newsweek* said that too); and that he'd acknowledged and taken responsibility for his error. Many defenders cited Buckley's answer to a question in a 2004 *Time* interview: "Have you taken any positions you now regret?" Buckley's answer: "Yes. I once believed we could evolve our way up from Jim Crow. I was wrong: federal intervention was necessary."

There Buckley admits to having been wrong about a position far different from the one he took in "Why the South Must Prevail," quoted above, which asserts a right—even a duty—of Southern whites to preserve Jim Crow, on the basis of the white race's supposedly greater advancement. Buckley's essay may strike readers today as typical of 1950s racist objections to civil-rights legislation. Its real impact lay in how sharply it departed from the typical, which can be revisited in a statement by Robert Byrd, today a U.S. Senator and in 1945 a twenty-eight-year-old member of the Ku Klux Klan. "Rather I should die a thousand times," young Byrd said, in the cadences that would later make him a darling of anti–Iraq War liberals, "and see Old Glory trampled in the dirt never to rise again, than to see this beloved land of ours become degraded by race mongrels, a throwback to the blackest specimen from the wilds." That comment appeared in a letter to the segregationist senator and former governor of Mississippi Theodore Bilbo, also a Klansman, who wrote a book entitled *Take Your Choice, Separation or Mongrelization* and filibustered an anti-lynching bill by invoking the "blood of the raped and outraged daughters of Dixie." (A period ditty sung by Pete Seeger was called "Listen,

Mr. Bilbo"—"Well, you don't like Negroes, you don't like Jews, / If there is anyone you do like, it sure is news.") Wearing white sheets and following Exalted Cyclopses and Grand Wizards, the Klan did not make sustained arguments in polished prose. As anti-intellectual as they were anti-black, Jim Crow supporters could be dismissed by educated liberals and made unappealing allies for educated conservatives.

Until the arrival of Buckley. His 1957 essay, a masterpiece of intellectual agility and verbal confidence, sounded like *The New Republic*, not *The Fiery Cross*. The essay's occasion was the recent success of Senate conservatives in preventing passage of legislation that would have required federal judges, not juries, to render verdicts in prosecutions of political operatives who failed to count black votes. The law was meant to hamper white juries' tendencies to free such defendants regardless of evidence. A striking feature of the essay is Buckley's outright support for jury nullification. Even more daringly he identifies a right for white Southerners, when in the minority, to "take such measures as are necessary to prevail." He presents that right as beyond the law, which he associates with "political abstractions," and beyond even the Constitution, which he calls not adequate to cope with issues raised by Jim Crow and the struggle against it.

Buckley is making the kind of "natural law" argument for rights transcending charter and legislation that late18th–century Americans made against the British Parliament's incursions on their liberties. It was a case that Bilbo and Byrd, sunk in hysteria and ignorance, needed a Yale man to make for them. Instead of denying or glossing over the consequence of the bill's defeat, Buckley announces it: "The effect of it is—and let us speak about it bluntly—to permit a jury to modify or waive the law." Buckley calls the supposed fact that whites are morally entitled to prevail by any means necessary a "sobering" one, admits that it is "unpleasant to adduce statistics" proving the white race superior (and does not actually do so), and appeals to the better angels of Southern nature, closing with a veiled threat that, if the South does not behave as Buckley expects it to, his support may have to be withdrawn:

> [The South] must not exploit the fact of Negro backwardness to preserve the Negro as a servile class. It is tempting and convenient to block the progress of a minority whose services, as menials, are economically useful. Let the South never permit itself to do this. So long as it is merely asserting the right to impose superior mores for whatever period it takes to effect a genuine cultural equality between the races, and so long as it does so by humane and charitable means, the South is in step with civilization, as is the Congress that permits it to function.

That is the evolution Buckley was calling for in 1957—not that "we could evolve our way up from Jim Crow," as he said in 2004, but that "the Negro" might, during some period determined and overseen by the superior race, evolve upward from the backwardness that had made Jim Crow not only permissible but necessary.

While this early entry is characteristic of Buckley's lifelong approach to argument, his fans and protégés cannot claim and celebrate it, because its most important theme—about which Buckley is also blunt, and which bears on his conservatism as a whole—comes down to the three-part statement that undergirds the essay and that few conservatives today would want to affirm:

> The claims of civilization supersede those of universal suffrage.... If the majority wills what is socially atavistic, then to thwart the majority may be, though undemocratic, enlightened.... sometimes the numerical minority cannot prevail except by violence: then it must determine whether the prevalence of its will is worth the terrible price of violence.

Civilization over democracy, even at the calculated, possibly tragic price of violence, taken up more in sorrow than in anger and then fought to the finish. That is the stance with which Buckley began creating a persona that may be unique in our cultural history. He ordained himself the leisure-class warrior-philosopher, provoked to militancy by ubiquitous barbarism, defending on behalf of conservatism not mere intellect but the highest cultural sophistication and refinement. That persona would make him not only a conservative leader but also a household name. On his TV show "Firing Line," which ran from 1966 to 1999, he did the Eastern establishment one better, at once a parody and epitome of upper-crust manner, with an over-the-top hot-potato drawl that made FDR sound salt-of-the-earth. Buckley's perfectly phrased insults and languorous polysyllabary made him the pop-culture model of intellectual, cultural, and verbal advancement, an unflappable connoisseur, guardian of the best ever thought and said by man. Delighting in the joys of rationality, beauty, hierarchy, imagination, humor, and awe, as expressed especially in the music of Bach, he seemed called from his fig tree by an Athenian sense of citizenship, battling to push back both the mob and the weak-willed mob-enablers who were ruining the civilization that had produced his own gorgeousness.

Hence a contradiction. It seems to have become evident to Buckley early on. Southern workingmen out to prevent "mongrelization" made poor exemplars of his ideas about advanced culture. Soon he was letting go of his hopes for the white South.

At a famous 1965 Oxford Union Debate with James Baldwin, for example, fighting what was already a rearguard action on civil rights, Buckley took the opportunity to argue against wholesale condemnation of American civilization for failing to live up to what Buckley now called its highest ideals. Averring that everybody agreed that race prejudice is evil, he accused the civil rights movement of no longer seeking equality but the actual regression of the white race (though he also continued to call slow progress on equal rights necessary); announced that if the issue must come to race war, he was prepared (echoing Churchill for his Oxonian audience) to fight it on the beaches, in the hills, in the mountains; and suggested, for a laugh, that what he really objected to was any uneducated Southerner, black or white, being allowed to vote. That joke distilled an unusual mix of states-rights populism and upper-class prerogative put forth at length, that same year, by James J. Kilpatrick in *National Review*: federalism will be destroyed unless states are free to impose voting qualifications, but those qualifications must discriminate equally, not on the basis of race.

It's not clear what refinements Buckley thought poor blacks and poor whites below the Mason-Dixon line should demonstrate, or be denied access to the franchise. What is clear is that Buckley's later thinking on integration was not, as his defenders claim, a turnabout on race itself but a retreat to a more logically consistent snobbism. *National Review* lost its all-out fights against school integration and the Voting Rights and Civil Rights Acts, but race long remained the defining conservative issue. Among many examples is a 1969 column in which Buckley hymned the research of Arthur Jensen on race and IQ, which showed blacks testing lower than whites on abstract reasoning skills, a finding from which Buckley deduced a racial imperviousness to improvement by education. In the 1970s *National Review* persistently defended apartheid South Africa on the same basis that it had once defended Jim Crow.

A legacy of Buckley's development on race is today's conservative opposition to programs like affirmative action. Nobody today bases that opposition on a duty to preserve white privilege and prevent anarchy. Opponents jump through hoops to show dedication to equality and democracy. Yet criticism of affirmative action, however altered its tone, is a direct inheritor of the ideological contributions Buckley made to conservatism in the 1950s. Today's position represents a fallback, not a break, from Buckley's ideas, which were never renounced, only defeated. The important issue is not the possible persistence of racist ideas in Buckley's own thinking, but modern conservatives' utter—and utterly convenient—expunging, when it comes to race, of the intellectual origins of modern conservatism.

SEEGER AND BUCKLEY WERE PUBLIC ROmantics. When they were young, and without regard for consequence, they brought charisma, energy, and creativity to dreaming up worlds they wanted—possibly needed—to live in. Because they made those worlds seem so real and beautiful that other people wanted to live in them too, they became larger-than-life characters, instantly recognizable a long way off, not quite real close up, and never quite grown up even when old. Hence their decisive influence. Seeger gave American folk music a purism in no way essential to it, a function of New England abstemiousness in Seeger's own makeup, which also connected him to Soviet communism. The Soviet Union is gone, but our music will never shake the purism. Seeger once said, with wit and accuracy, "I'm more conservative than Goldwater. He just wanted to turn the clock back to when there was no income tax. I want to turn the clock back to when people lived in small villages and took care of each other." Those yearnings began in his father's dreams for the future, but it was a dream about the past that made him Pete Seeger. In Buckley's dream, somebody is going to live in the castle above the village—better for everybody that it be he. That each in his own way dreamed southward, with fateful results, made them public romantics in a special American tradition.

An important difference between Seeger and Buckley is that Seeger suffered for his beliefs. The film's pose of innocence about his Stalinist provocations aside, he bravely risked jail by refusing to answer some of HUAC's questions; he was blacklisted, his career ruined for a long time. The film shows his concerts being angrily picketed by Young Americans for Freedom—Buckley's organization. Yet even in Seeger's persecution lies a telling reminder of what the two men shared: a sense that there are certain rights of which only the questing individual himself can be arbiter. When refusing to give names to HUAC, Seeger chose not to rely on his Fifth Amendment right against self-incrimination, claiming instead a transcendent liberty, that of association, which he could not prove but believed was natural, pre-dating any claims made by a committee of federal government.

Liberals may concur in calling Seeger's Stalinism romantic, if unfortunate (although *American Masters* viewers are not supposed to; the Stalinism is not supposed to exist). But liberals may also feel that "romantic" softens the virulence of Buckley's race ideas, letting him off too easily. Buckleyites, for their part, cannot call segregationism romantic, since they have left its central importance out of their story—and they are likely to feel that the adjective understates the evil done by Seeger's Soviet loyalties. Each side in this story has become adept not only at falsifying its own narrative but also at picking apart the other's fallacies to expose venal motives. It is unfortunate that each side, in accusing the other of bad faith, so often seems to be right.

Buckley's and Seeger's shared attraction to extremes did have the effect of condoning awful crimes: lynching of blacks and murder of civil-rights workers on the one hand, Stalin's mass murder on the other. Sorting out kinds and degrees of awfulness is as problematic as determining whether condoning those crimes also contributed to them. (The men themselves remained professionally innocent.) More important is that the two were far from alone. For if their dreams were not our dreams, too, we would never have heard the names Pete Seeger and William F. Buckley, Jr.

3
Constitutional Conventions

In East Berlin, the Memorial to the Victims of Fascism and Militarism was a big attraction. Soviet-bloc tourists mobbed it, and by the mid-1980s visitors also included NATO-country citizens on day-pass jaunts over the famous wall. Built as the New Guard House of Friedrich Wilhelm III, the Memorial had neoclassical, Doric-style columns under a low-peaked pediment. Within its echoing dimness, a clear prismatic block, Soviet-moderne, fragmented an eternal flame.

The draw was the changing of the guard out front. Orders were shrieked as young soldiers goose-stepped through a routine. You might see two of them, seemingly identical under their helmets, crack a surreptitious joke as one presented arms to the other. The crowd, nearly silent only moments before, surged abruptly toward the stamping boots to get a better look, while a line of police, as young and ostentatiously armed as the guards, swung truncheons, yelled, pushed the crowd back with viciously barking dogs. People in the crowd laughed, fell back, pushed forward.

The Memorial to the Victims of Fascism and Militarism gave chilling summation to the totalitarianism that had created it, in part because of its outrageous contradiction—claiming to condemn historic evils while making a triumphant display of them—and even more profoundly because the contradiction didn't seem to be on anybody's mind. In the liberal imagination, that sort of bald falsehood is supposed to invite public mockery, ultimately public rejection. And it is true that the wall came down. The so-called German Democratic Republic is no more.

Sightseers weren't brainwashed into thinking military exercise is fitting remembrance of victims of militarism. Nor did they think police swinging sticks were harmless. They might have been thinking all kinds of things. Thinking was beside the point. In that sense the Memorial only took public history to its most grotesque extreme. From the Parthenon to Trafalgar Square, from the bronze Andrew Jackson of New Orleans to the gilded General Sherman of New York, from Arthurian legend to Serbian epic, history geared for a whole people usually celebrates founding moments, famous victories, hair's-breadth escapes, tragic losses. It does not always promote fascism. It does tend, almost by definition, to rally nationalism. Thought and nuanced feeling get stifled.

In a real democratic republic, where the whole people is supposed to be required to think, a different kind of public history is needed—lively and accessible, yet able to inspire without falsifying and to encourage consideration along with awe. So it is a deeply unhappy irony that the National Constitution Center in Philadelphia, which since 2003 has celebrated on a grand scale our founding moment and enduring national law, obliterates dissent and pushes foregone and even false conclusions on its visitors. Undermining its own insistence on the importance of democracy to the United States, the Constitution Center reveals how readily public curators, even if well-meaning, may seek to control rather than foster thought.

THE FIRST IMPRESSION the Constitution Center makes is sheer size. Approaching from a distance on Independence Mall, you confront a high stone curtain against blank sky. The façade eschews any kitschy colonial or federal-era references. This is a temple—grave, stirring, and monumental. No one pretends anything happened here.

The next impression is a strange emptiness. On a Sunday morning last spring, there was no line for the Constitution Center. Other attractions on the mall's almost treeless expanse were drawing families of avid American-history tourists, splashes of color against the green. Near the south end of the mall sits the eighteenth-century Pennsylvania State House, with its famous cupola and bell tower (because the U.S. Constitution and the Declaration of Independence were debated and signed there, it has been known for years as Independence Hall). Strung along the mall's western edge are the National Park Service's Visitor Center and the Liberty Bell's low-slung viewing house. The eastern edge opens on the preserved and reconstructed old city—Carpenter's Hall, and the site of Benjamin Franklin's home, and brick buildings and gardens with appeal for history buffs and old-house fans alike. The imposing Constitution Center walls off the north end.

That Sunday morning the tourists were already walking the shady streets, booking tickets for the ranger-guided tours of Independence Hall, and lining up for the Liberty Bell. Once the few people hanging around outside the Constitution Center went in, the building looked eerily still. In the Center's vast lobby, filled with natural light, emptiness expands. The ceiling soars with vaulting tetrahedrons. Visitors pass an elderly greeter evincing vague cheer in Wal-Mart mode and wander toward a distant ticket-booth island, wondering aloud what's up, since there's almost nothing to see but plaques praising private donors ("Patriots," "Founders," etc.) and a staircase sweeping to a broad, curving mezzanine lined by full-scale state flags hanging from the high ceiling. At the booth you and your fellow visitors are reminded that unlike National Park Service sites, where admission is included in your tax obligation, the Center charges. The ticket, almost as large as an open billfold, is an important-looking souvenir labeled "Delegate's Pass"; you also get a red-white-and-blue paper wristband like those for drink tickets. But there's still no visible enticement or obvious place to go. Friendly young ticket-sellers mention casually that the next show will start soon. Visitors gather that they're supposed to see it. Another young employee stands in the distance, waiting to take part of the ticket. You troop past her.

You've entered a circular hall surrounding a cylindrical theater. While waiting for doors in the inner wall to open to the theater, you wander the circle, whose other wall is dedicated to impressionistic street scenes and maps of Philadelphia in 1787, year of the Constitutional Convention. Amid recorded bird chirping and period street noise, disembodied voices give actor-y exposition. "I grant you that times are bad, but . . ." "Have you seen the latest broadside by our friend Jupiter Howard of Long Island? . . ." The theater doors fly open automatically. You leave the eighteenth century and enter a dim space with steeply banked, industrial-chic seats around a circle of floor, where a presenter will stand and speak in the round.

During several visits, the seats were far from full. Once there seemed to be fewer than fifteen people scattered about the dark. A collage of period music and noise—bagpipes, clopping hooves, hymns, fiddles and fifes, black worksongs—is interrupted periodically by a recorded announcement of welcome, instruction, and prohibition: no eating or drinking, leave at the end of the show by going up the stairs, not through the lower entrances, etc. The coolly comforting female voice repeating the message, the automatically opening doors, and the podlike ambience make the place feel 1960s-futuristic.

The young workers close the doors. Lights dim further. The presenter enters through the last open door—that Sunday an African-American woman in a trim, man-cut dark suit and open-necked white shirt. A light shines brightly on her as she takes the center of the floor. "We . . . the *people*," she begins, looking around at the spectators. Her voice and face blend immense wonder, delight, and curiosity. She has a big job to do. The presentation rests on her delivery of a script, supported by music and sound and by imagery on a cyclorama running around the top of the theater.

The show is called "Freedom Rising," and the presenter channels its relentless mood of triumph through facial expression, phrasing, and dynamics. This kind of recitation, with every gesture and glance memorized and controlled, was once an important part of American entertainment. The presenter is amplified, but her style is pre-amplification, pitched for the outdoor platform, the revue hall, the pulpit, and for an era when audiences with high tolerance for artificiality delighted in vocal nuance and expressive gesture. Near the climax, having asked rhetorically what will keep us together as a nation, the presenter starts pointing at various members of the audience, making eye contact and answering her own question: "You, sir . . . and you . . . and you . . . and you!" By the end she's shouting her story, having climbed to an upper aisle, while images flash around the high cyclorama and the music swells over military drumbeat. The cyclorama is pulling your gaze upward. Soaring music and rhetoric make you feel, willy-nilly, as if you are lifting your head not to see, but nobly, eyes fixed on an ideal about which you feel increasingly fervent. Whatever you may really be thinking, participation is made physical. "You!" are no mere spectator. "You!" are the star player in a thrilling historical tableau.

WHICH IS THE WHOLE POINT. AT THE Constitution Center, democracy and the U.S. Constitution are synonymous. The Center makes the first three words of the document's preamble, "We, the people," both its theme and its brand. The Center's tagline is "The

Story of We, the People." And during last year's election season, a special exhibit in the entry hall, swallowed by the surrounding emptiness, was entitled, awkwardly, "The Power of We." It consisted of big cutouts of Barack Obama and John McCain for photo-ops, a fast-moving LED-countdown to Election Day, and an invitation to write down a sentence you'd like to hear in the new president's inaugural address. ("I'm thinking Arby's," someone suggested.) At every moment, the Center frames "We" as a gathering in nationhood of the sort of ordinary, well-intentioned people who visit the Center, and from whose democratic spirit the Constitution has drawn, from the founding moment onward, history-changing power.

After "Freedom Rising" has identified "you!" as the main actor in "We," it's time for the next step. Amid desultory applause, the audience is again reminded to leave not by the doors at floor level but by mounting to doors around the aisle above the seats, as the next group is herded in. Outside the upper doors, you find yourself in a wide museum exhibit space encircling the top of the theater cylinder. In contrast to the proscriptions and forced emotion of the theater experience, here you're turned entirely loose on a set of exhibits of the kind known to museum-goers as interactive.

Interactivity in museum exhibits is commonly described as democratizing. Instead of gazing at a work and reading a trained curator's remarks about it, the interacting visitor contributes and completes. That idea is as old as the Metropolitan Museum's Temple of Dendur and the Cloisters, where inhabiting a space is meant to enliven seeing and knowing. The full-scale, high-tech version is usually found not in art museums but in halls of fame and other centers for history, science, and culture not meant only for contemplation, needing imaginative, accessible ways of informing and inspiring.

The democratizing effect of interactive media might seem especially useful to a museum dedicated to what it claims is the archetypal narrative of democracy itself, with the ordinary person as chief actor. But at the Constitution Center, in the absence of any guidance, structure, or starting point, the freedom quickly becomes chaos. Here the "multimedia" that usually accompanies interactive museum exhibits means loud, distorted playback of recorded sound from many video monitors. Each soundtrack clashes and overlaps with others. Kids run to an exhibit to see what it does, then run to the next. Some adults take more time, especially with what turns out to be a set of displays reviewing Constitutional history from the confederation period to September 11, 2001, running in cases all the way along one wall. But there is at once too much to see in those cases and too little focus or substance, even for patient and interested visitors.

Meanwhile, with cacophonous interactivity, the Center is trying hard to dramatize its "We"/"you!" theme, the centrality of the ordinary person in giving life to the Constitution. Yet the exhibits are insipid. You're provided with paper and pencil and prompted to write down what it means to be an American. You can vote for your favorite president: kids seem to like this setup, which involves mock voting booths and a staged "election night" TV report on video monitors above the booths, where a correspondent excitedly interviews pundits—which president will emerge tonight's winner?—who turn out to be Gordon Wood and Richard Beeman, major real-life historians. (Wood notes in passing that the presidency was modeled on the eighteenth-century monarchy. It's hard to hear, but nobody's listening anyway.)

The importance of "you!" is taken to fantastic lengths in another bit, where visitors get sworn in as president. A faux chief justice on video, oddly depressed-looking, intones each phrase of the oath in the general direction of a space monitored by a closed-circuit camera.

If you step into that space, another monitor displays you and the judge together, and you repeat after him. Teenagers throng to get sworn in together, laughing uproariously, pressing a button to interrupt the process and start over. Meanwhile TV personality Ben Stein is answering mailed-in questions about the Constitution on a giant video monitor; there's a jury box to sit in (because juries were invented by the U.S. Constitution?); there's a towering sculpture made only of law books. It doesn't do anything. One exhibit that draws kids only to disappoint them is a giant sculpture that resembles a Mattel "Hot Wheels" set: chrome roadways twist and turn with model cars and trucks stuck to them, while traffic roars. Nothing moves. Instead, on a crumpled surface resembling a loading-dock floor, you turn wheels to reveal fiscal data about state, local, and federal responsibilities for the nation's highways.

Moving toward the exit takes you through "Signers' Hall." Standing around this big room are statues of the Constitution's framers, exactly life-sized and perfectly proportioned, frozen chatting with one another in pairs and groups. Are these ghosts, visiting our world? Are we flashing back to theirs? In any event, we're all milling about together, famous founders and ordinary folk (in contrast to the real convention, which was kept so secret that windows to the chamber were sealed). Sidle up to Ben Franklin, drape an arm around Alexander Hamilton, get a grinning group snapshot with George Washington. They and "you!" mingle freely on equal terms. The Constitution's essentially democratic nature is again made physical.

With nothing left to do, you leave Signers' Hall and find yourself on the broad mezzanine above the entrance hall. Vacant space curves around to the grand staircase back down to the lobby. Along this gallery hang those huge state flags, with dates of admission to the Union. For some reason there are also three video monitors high on a wall. They showed one day: C-SPAN, a tout to support the Center, and, no doubt inadvertently, the E! Channel, which happened to be airing the movie *Showgirls*.

What has inspired this mix of lavishness and shabbiness? Why is it so empty, in every sense of the word? Poor attendance gives a weird quality to both the hyper-controlled "Freedom Rising" show and the chaotic exhibit hall. The effort is flat-out indoctrination—yet nobody seems very interested. One might dismiss the whole thing as merely cheesy and dumb. But weak aesthetics and an apparent lack of operational precision are belied by the passion, prestige, and money that went into the Center's creation. Somebody wanted this gigantic footprint to make a historical statement. The building's assertive placement and modernist grandeur elevate the formerly underrated importance of the 1787 signing of the Constitution, counterbalancing the old site at the mall's other end, whose name emphasizes the spirit of 1776 and American independence. Plaques off the lobby reveal that major figures in the studies of history and law are committed to the Center's success. The Distinguished Scholars Advisory Panel is headed by professors Wood and Beeman. The Stanford Law Dean Kathleen Sullivan is typical of the big names in Constitutional law that grace the Panel. John Yoo joined when he was known as a conservative Berkeley law professor; he later gained notoriety in President Bush's Office of Legal Counsel.

What did such high-profile, well-connected people of varying political leanings hope the National Constitution Center would become? What sort of programs did they imagine it presenting? At every turn, the Center breathlessly insists that "you!" are at once empowered and relied on, that every American is embraced, in a way unknown elsewhere, by "We." Insistence keeps taking the form of pandering, flattering, and rallying, and it keeps falling flat.

The real problem may not be with the Constitution Center. It may be with the Constitution itself.

ONE OF THE DEEPEST TENSIONS IN PUBLIC thinking about the Constitution can be felt in the role that race plays in the Center's narratives. Those narratives encapsulate for the general public what scholars know as a "consensus" reading of American history (though many reject the category as simplistic). The term has various meanings and shadings, but refers generally, as its name suggests, to shared American values, transcending political divides and social conflicts and making us, for all our differences, one nation. Breathlessness about the Constitution is a fairly crude manifestation of the consensus approach, which involves more than mere admiration. It has been supported by many of our more sophisticated historians, who argue that the Constitution put into legal operation essentially American commitments and attitudes, which, despite flaws and setbacks, tend to endow more and more people with freedom and equality.

Consensus history thus gives intellectual underpinning to an American liberalism that many self-described conservatives espouse as well. No serious presidential candidate, whatever he plans to do in office, questions the historical consensus, which is ultimately positive, ready-made for the sound bite, and by definition widely accepted. Most candidates, however, give consensus only a reflexive nod. A closer look tends to uncover conflicts. It was an important moment not only for race relations but also for public attitudes about founding history when Barack Obama did far more than merely acknowledge the consensus reading of American history.

Obama gave his famous speech on race at the Constitution Center. The speech's title, "A More Perfect Union," is drawn from the phrase of the preamble following "We, the people," and its approach to history tracks the narrative dramatized at the Center. In his opening, Obama described the signers, fancifully, as a roomful of men who "had traveled across an ocean to escape tyranny and persecution." They "finally made real their declaration of independence" by devising and signing the Constitution and creating a nation. That picture makes the Constitution an expression of fundamental American ideas about liberty and equality, first put in practice, supposedly imperfectly, in the confederation of states that prevailed from 1776 to 1787, and given reality and stability only in the signing of the Constitution and the making of national government.

"Freedom Rising" tells that story too; fulsomely, so less believably. By the end of the show, the script has credited the Constitution with enabling "community"—"the day-to-day life of 'We, the people,'" the presenter says—as if even day-to-day life had been waiting for the signing to come into being. A translucent box descends from the ceiling and encases the presenter while she invokes the likes of Duke Ellington and Louis Armstrong, whose pictures are projected on the box's scrim. Elvis gets there too: without the signers, no rock and roll. Projections and sound bites feature FDR, World War II, and Ronald Reagan telling Gorbachev to tear down that Wall. Even Richard Nixon does his bit, just by resigning. Gerald Ford is heard reminding us that "our Constitution works."

The "stain," as Obama and others have put it, on all that otherwise untarnished national glory is slavery. In "Freedom Rising," the subject gets a special moment. "Slavery . . . !" the presenter intones grimly; the music slows, becomes moody. But unlike Obama's far more forthright reading, which demands that we think about race itself, the "Freedom Rising" script somehow manages to avoid using the words "African" or "black" in connection with slavery. We hear only about "enslaved people."

We're also reminded that slavery had long been a feature of civilization, and that the signers were "desperate" to create a nation. So with the stain acknowledged, it's right back to the uplift, and because the story now becomes one of greater and greater inclusion, the mood can remain untouched by what we've just been supposed to consider. The exhibit hall, with more ample chronology, does tell of setbacks and struggles from slavery to civil rights and beyond. But there, too, social progress is presented as inevitable because based on the Constitution, which spreads a fundamentally American democracy throughout America and the world, qualified by one stain and one stain only.

With everybody appearing to have considered, as one, the horror of the stain, the consensus holds. Does it hold, in that sense, because of the stain? Obama's "A More Perfect Union," having laid strong claim to the consensus, made more trenchant and challenging points about the harrowing effects of slavery and racism in

America than the Constitution Center's narratives probably ever will. Yet Obama's challenge, too, rests on unshakable faith in a fundamentally American ethos supposedly at work, albeit imperfectly, in the signing. Celebrating a democratic national consensus, "We" get together and give ourselves goosebumps.

You wouldn't know it by listening to campaign speeches or by visiting the Constitution Center, but there is no agreement about consensus history or the democratic purpose of the Constitution. A hundred-year war rages in history circles over what was really going on at the founding when it comes to equality, liberty, and law, and how those relationships affected the writing and ratification of the Constitution we live by every day. This war stays out of public view in part because it does not turn solely on issues made notorious in recent decades as "multicultural"—slavery, female disenfranchisement, race and gender inequality;

also the ignored contributions of women and minorities—or, at the other end of the scale, on conservative philosophies like "originalism," in Justice Scalia's preferred term, where interpretations that promote social progress are deemed outright distortions of Constitutional intent. Those dissents are famous. This war involves facts even more deeply disturbing to our shared faith in the American values of the founding moment.

Delegates came to Philadelphia in 1787 not to form a democracy but to redress "insufficient checks against the democracy," as Edmund Randolph of Virginia put it in his opening remarks, which framed the convention's agenda. Both Alexander Hamilton, representing New York, and Elbridge Gerry of Massachusetts, sworn enemies, rallied fellow delegates to rein in "an excess of democracy" by forming a national government. It is sheer fantasy to say that, having been shakily established in the Declaration, "democracy stumbled" (as "Freedom Rising" puts it) during the confederation period, and so had to be restored for all time by the Constitution. To the delegates, precisely the reverse was true. Rivalries that flourished before and after the convention—Southern planters vs. urban financiers; nationalists vs. state-sovereigntists—were subsumed in a common effort to push democracy back. Those men chatting in Signers' Hall weren't keeping women and minorities out of an otherwise democratic republic. They were framing a republic to limit the democracy recently taken up by white men.

If those remarks sound novel and bizarre, that's the novel and bizarre thing. Such a critique once enjoyed wide currency, and though little discussed publicly now, continues to be part and parcel of all serious, informed debate about American founding history. Today's consensus historians—towering examples include Wood (co-chair of the Constitution Center's Advisory Panel), an eminent professor of history at Brown, and Edmund Morgan, professor emeritus at Yale—achieved their success by addressing the obduracy of those facts about the founders' efforts. They have opposed the long sway of a competing historical viewpoint, anticonsensus, put forth by scholars like Charles Beard, Carl Becker, and Merrill Jensen, "progressive historians" whose reputations have declined. In the first part of the last century, the progressive historians looked closely and publicly at the signers' elitism; the powerful democratic impulses and activities of ordinary, less-enfranchised white men; troubled relationships among political equality, economic fairness, and liberty; entrenched sectional conflicts; and the question of whether the framers were constituting a national government, at least in part, as a counterrevolution to shore up elite interests.

Those historians focused, in other words, on class. They found themselves at least as interested in a founding struggle among Americans as in a founding struggle against the British Empire. Some of them saw the founders' opposition to democracy arising from financial self-interest, which the signers pursued by constituting a national government that favored elite interests. Some of the progressive historians could be baldly elitist themselves; some tried to locate anti-elitism in unlikely places.

Like all schools of thought, the progressives made many now-evident mistakes, were excessively influenced by social and political trends, and fell out of favor when moods changed. Amid new moods, and with new scholarly arsenals, the consensus historians who absorbed and surpassed them have rejected class warfare among Americans as a fundamental element in the founding story. In the academy, certain developments of progressive-history assumptions do thrive—right-wingers complain they even rule—but in public history, quashing class interpretations of the founding period has been decisive not because the public has been persuaded, after careful thought, that class turns out not to be important to the founding after all, but because the public mind seems committed to not thinking about class. The unfortunate result is the absence of any realism, at the Constitution Center and elsewhere, about founding purposes.

Yet the historians who enable the assumptions most convenient to cheap celebration are not themselves cheap. They are among our most adept and learned professors, with the highest-profile careers, often admirably committed to writing both for peers and for general readers. Nor do they march in lock step. Scholarship has led each to a personal interpretation. Edmund Morgan, for example, now in his nineties, embodies the centrist liberalism of the consensus view. Among the best-known of his many important works are the scholarly yet readable *The Stamp Act Crisis*, *The Puritan Dilemma*, and *American Slavery, American Freedom*, as well as a lucid overview for general readers, *The Birth of the Republic*.

Early on Morgan defined his intellectual enemies as, on the one hand, revisionist neo-Tory historians who were questioning the purity of the American tax resisters' motives, and on the other, American progressives like Beard, who seemed to ascribe venal financial self-interest to the Constitution's framers.

Morgan built a body of work dedicated to showing utter consistency of principle on the part of American patriots, from the first protests through ratification. His sensibility, and that of the informed consensus as a whole, may be glimpsed in this remark from *The Birth of the Republic*, in which he acknowledges the self-interest Beard had pointed to, while absorbing it in an optimistic consensus reading:

> In each case self-interest led to the enunciation of principles which went far beyond the point at issue. In each case the people of the United States were committed to doctrines which helped to mold their future in ways they could

not have anticipated. At the Constitutional Convention much the same thing occurred. The members had a selfish interest in bringing about a public good.

Gordon Wood, a generation younger than Morgan, follows some of the old progressives in defining the American Revolution as socially radical. Wood means by "radical" something different from what leftists mean. In *The Radicalism of the American Revolution*, as well as in many engaging articles for *The New York Review of Books*, Wood has put a wide frame around the founding. For him the Revolution was not accomplished until the age of Jackson, when social mobility, small-scale enterprise, and a rowdy, unrefined spirit brought America into its own. Wood sees true American radicalism not in any failed or suppressed effort at populist egalitarianism, but in ending traditional forms of social deference and making a dynamic modern society. He doesn't need to explain away the elitism of the famous founders, which had once led him, in progressive vein, to label the Constitution "aristocratic." In Wood's most mature work, the Revolution didn't end until those founders had been left behind and America had settled on the reasonably liberal, restlessly capitalist, socially fluid society that eighteenth-century citizens wouldn't have recognized.

For all the provocative nuance possible within the consensus, its tendency is to give the public a false impression that any discomfiting ideas about the role of class in our founding have been permanently superseded by more judicious, less partial scholarship. There is in fact a persuasive competing view, presented with great verve and insight by historians associated with the New Left—Jesse Lemisch, Staughton Lynd, Dirk Hoerder, and others. They have uncovered the eighteenth-century radical movement of ordinary and unenfranchised people who equated democracy with legislating social fairness and forcefully dissented, often with rowdy crowd actions, from elite monetary policy and unfettered capitalism alike. Consensus historians define such movements as anachronistic, at best marginal. That's a soothing notion for more-or-less liberal middle-class history buffs. It also gives support to the deadening self-congratulation and outright falsehood on display at the Constitution Center. In academic history, a consensus view may be arrived at. In public history, consensus is coerced.

So complete, in fact, is the public success of the consensus view that smart new books hoping to shake it up for general readers are not widely known. The one book on the Constitution that has enjoyed strong sales in recent years is *America's Constitution: A Biography* by Akhil Reed Amar, a thick consensus work, leading the reader through a familiar if unusually detailed celebration of the document as establishing unprecedented degrees of popular sovereignty.

The press has largely ignored neo-progressive books that anyone interested in the story behind the Constitution would also have to read, books that offer fresh, well-argued challenges to the notion that the famous founders were motivated by democratic instincts, or that their work tended inevitably toward democracy regardless of their instincts.

Some of the best are Terry Bouton's *Taming Democracy* and Woody Holton's *Unruly Americans and the Origins of the Constitution*. Gary Nash's *The Unknown American Revolution*, another work of lively dissent, actually did get some attention—even some criticism from the consensus side—and is available, pleasingly enough, in some history-tourism gift shops (though not at the Constitution Center's).

Is it imaginable that any history-tourism destination would want to admit complexities that might send visitors home more troubled than satisfied, more questioning than answered, wondering how we got here, where we're going, and what it would take to develop a personal point of view on the whole thing?

Possibly not—but if John Yoo, Bush White House apparatchik, can share space on the Constitution Center's Advisory Panel with Gordon Wood, why can't a neo-progressive like Woody Holton, whose book, though little-known, was a finalist for the National Book Award? A less stiff and pushy presentation than "Freedom Rising," fired by competing ideas, might dispense with hand-on-heart nation-worship and find some real drama—even suspense—in the opposition to the Constitution that prevailed during the founding, from the planter elitism of Patrick Henry, who identified liberty with the sovereignty of Virginia, to the rugged egalitarianism of little-known, equally idiosyncratic elected leaders, like the Pennsylvania farmer Robert Whitehill and the backcountry preacher Herman Husband, who objected not to national government itself but to what they saw as the Constitution's suppression of working-class democracy. Greater forthrightness about slavery and less patronizing squeamishness about race would also help liven things up.

Ideas for exhibits might be sparked by unyoking the user-centric nature of interactive functionality from the one-note message that the country, too, is by nature user-centric. Some way of re-devising the more startling solutions proposed and fought over by the convention delegates (and quickly passed over by "Freedom Rising" as if manifestly absurd)—obliteration of the states, limited monarchy, unicameral legislature—could be both fun and informative. Even a video showing consensus and anti-consensus scholars hotly debating the real meaning of the Constitution would be more compelling and incisive than Ben Stein talking to a camera.

Debate, which gave rise to the Constitution, and which it protects, is what's really missing from the Center. Where better to hold public discussion of, for example, the surveillance camera visible in the Independence Hall belltower, commanding the mall from where the Liberty Bell once rang? If calling the place Independence Hall now differs appreciably from calling snapping guard dogs and goose-stepping troops a Memorial to the Victims of Fascism and Militarism, it would be reassuring to hear why, and to hear it at a place dedicated to constitutional issues.

What the Constitution Center keeps trying to beat into our heads is that our nation differs categorically from all others. But national identity always claims categorical difference. To make an American difference real and believable would mean actually doing something different—and that would mean expecting more from "We, the people" than the desire to push a button and admire ourselves, yet again, on video. Some of the founders were suspicious of democracy because they viewed the mass of American people as incapable of making independent judgments. Overbearing national narratives try to rob people of that capacity, abusing both history and the citizens who come, of their own free will, to learn about it.

So it makes a pleasant change, after visiting the Constitution Center, to walk the length of the mall to Independence Hall. National Park Service rangers give tours on a demanding schedule, and while things move along briskly, each tour has a different quality, because each ranger is passionately informed. After looking around the State House yard, where mass meetings took place throughout the eighteenth century, and before entering the chamber that the Pennsylvania Assembly loaned to delegates of the Second Continental Congress, and then, eleven years later, to those of the Constitutional Convention, each tour group gathers for a few moments of orientation. The rangers ask some basic questions, and handle without condescension responses that show a wide range of historical interest and sophistication within any one group and from group to group. The rangers are not delving into a lot of dissenting history. We're all in the group for our own reasons, and it turns out to be somebody's job—our federal government's!—to help us gain whatever degree of understanding we seek.

Something big did happen a long time ago, twice, in this building. It's good to stand again in the old chamber, always surprisingly small, and remember that it was real.

ACKNOWLEDGEMENTS

THANKS TO DEBORAH CHASMAN AND Joshua Cohen of *Boston Review* for rare astuteness and sympathy in editing, which has helped shape my writing and my subject. *BR* Managing Editor Simon Waxman's diligence and insight have contributed much to the making of this book; thanks as well to former *BR* Managing Editor Catherine Tumber. My wife, Gail Brousal, made important early-draft suggestions about all three pieces. Bob Bender and Eric Lupfer gave important help. Thanks to George Restrepo for beautiful cover art. And thanks to Clay Morgan and all others at MIT Press who helped create this book.

A number of people offered expressions of support; a number have engaged in illuminating conversation and correspondence. I bring them all together here, with gratitude (and no implication in anything I've said): Clarissa Atkinson, Dean Baker, Daniel Bergner, David Boaz, Terry Bouton, Christopher Caldwell, Steve Clemons, William Everdell, Kyle Gann, Doug Harvey, Wythe Holt, Jesse Lemisch, Barry Lynn, Paul O'Rourke, Jeffrey Pasley, Rick Perlstein, Eleanor Shakin, Sam Sifton, Kip Voytek, Mike Wallace, Jon Wiener, and Frank Wilkinson. I've appreciated support, challenges, and publicity from bloggers and journalists, including 3QuarksDaily, Andrew Sullivan, Arts & Letters Daily, Boston 1775, Brian Doherty, The Brothers Judd, Cato on Campus, History News Network, Lew Rockwell, Publick Occurrences, Rad Geek People's Daily, Ron Rosenbaum, and Progressive Historians. Thanks as well to the commenters on the *BR* Web site who caught gaffes and raised questions.

The deepest thanks go to my family.
WH

BOSTON REVIEW BOOKS

Boston Review Books is an imprint of *Boston Review*, a bimonthly magazine of ideas. The book series, like the magazine, is animated by hope, committed to equality, and convinced that the imagination eludes political categories. Visit bostonreview.net for more information.

The End of the Wild   STEPHEN M. MEYER

God and the Welfare State   LEW DALY

Making Aid Work   ABHIJIT VINAYAK BANERJEE

The Story of Cruel and Unusual   COLIN DAYAN

What We Know About Climate Change   KERRY EMANUEL

Movies and the Moral Adventure of Life   ALAN A. STONE

The Road to Democracy in Iran   AKBAR GANJI

Why Nuclear Disarmament Matters   HANS BLIX

Race, Incarceration, and American Values   GLENN C. LOURY

The Men in My Life   VIVIAN GORNICK

Africa's Turn?   EDWARD MIGUEL

Inventing American History   WILLIAM HOGELAND